I0802565

Introduction by W. Terrence Gordon

The Argument: Causality in the Electric World, by Marshall McLuhan and Barrington Nevitt, appeared originally in *Technology and Culture*, Vol. 14, #1 (University of Chicago Press, January, 1973), pp. 1-18. McLuhan and Nevitt had already collaborated to produce *Take Today: The Executive as Dropout* (Toronto: Longman, 1972). Here they reprise both themes from the book and from McLuhan's publications spanning twenty years, offering much fresh material by constantly linking those themes to the notion of causality. With reinforcement from James Joyce, they comment on the ancient Greeks transforming their cosmos into an ordered figure against the old ground of 'chaotic' change, leading Western philosophers to take the abstract figure of Greek Nature as an artificial ground cut into conceptual figures obscuring existence. With reinforcement from Harold Innis, this is linked to the separation of cause from effect. Later, the perennially favorite McLuhan topic of advertising is also integrated with figure/ground analysis: "Even the ad agencies know that to sell a car or a coat they must present the satisfactions in figure-ground relationship that will create the desired psychic effects." Because effects are perceived, while causes are conceived, McLuhan and Nevitt can sweep away the conventional ideas of evolution and technology as illusions engendered by the visual bias of literate cultures. They also add dimensions of meaning to the notion of medium as message: "Experiments designed to confirm the old normally conceal the new," expanding on this observation as follows: "When we say 'the medium is the message,' we suppress the fact that the user or audience or cognitive agent is both the 'content' and maker of the experience, in order to highlight the effects of the medium or the hidden environment or ground of the experience." In the insistence on the inseparability between the dualities cause/effect and figure/ground that constitutes the unifying thread of this essay, it is possible to detect a corrective for the excesses and abuses of a major current in modern thought: “We are often smothered in images of ourselves and of others that do not correspond to ‘presences.’ The Western world has built up a vast apparatus of classifications as a means of controlling and harmonizing experience. These have tended to be collosal systems of concepts which prevent us from direct encounter with ourselves and our world: they constitute the ‘rear-view mirror.’ But existentialism pushed to extreme as a figure loses touch with the ground of existence itself.” — WTG

The Argument: Causality in the Electric World –

Marshall McLuhan & Barrington Nevitt

The situation is complicated and its difficulties are enhanced by the impossibility of saying everything at once.[1]

In today's ECO-world of electric information that flows unceasingly upon us from every side, we all encounter the predicament of Alice in Wonderland. Now effects merge with causes instantly through speedup, while "software" etherializes "hardware" by design.[2] All rigid distinctions between thinker and doer, observer and observed, object and subject are being eroded by the

1 R. T. Hersh citing Woodger on *Alice in Wonderland* in *American Scientist* (May-June, 1971), p. 293.

2 "Software" is the organization of information for the shaping and metamorphosis of its "hardware" embodiment. The hardware/software relationship is not fixed, but is constantly changing in the process of "etherialization" — doing more and more with less and less.

"rim-spin" of electric media. Old ground rules and human perceptions are being transformed by this new resonant surround where nothing is stable but change itself. But like water to a fish, the environment we live in remains hidden. Only children and artists see "the emperor's new clothes."

Continuity in Discontinuity

Today, metamorphosis by *chiasmus* — the reversal-of-process caused by increasing its speed, scope, or size — is visible everywhere for anyone to see. The chiasmus of speedup is slowdown. Perhaps first noted by ancient Chinese sages in I *Ching* or *The Book of Changes*, the history of chiastic patterns is traced through classical Greek and Hebrew literature by Nils W. Lund in *Chiasmus in the New Testament.*[3] Computer programmers have also learned that "information overload leads to pattern recognition" as breakdown becomes breakthrough: from "bits" to "bytes" to "whole" again.

Speeding up the components of any visually ordered structure or continuous space pattern will lead to breaking its connections and destroying its boundaries. They explode into the resonant gaps or interfaces that characterize the discontinuous structure of acoustic space. The visual perspective becomes an acoustic wraparound. Repetition of any visual pattern or modular form creates a mosaic with nonvisual effects, as the single photographic point of view becomes a multiple, iconic re-presentation. History becomes "mythic" through time-compression and juxtaposition of events as past, present, and future merge in electric nowness.

---

3 Chapel Hill, N. C., 1942.

Novelty Causes Antiquity

Every innovation, whether of "hardware" product or "software" information, is an extension of man. Novelty becomes cliché through use. And constant use creates a new hidden environment while simultaneously pushing the old invisible ground into prominence, as a new figure, clearly visible for the first time. Every innovation scraps its immediate predecessor and retrieves still older figures; it causes floods of antiques or nostalgic art forms and stimulates the search for "museum pieces." In such cliché-archetype patterns, the new continually recreates the old as novelty regenerates antiquity. Ancient cults and old jalopies are revived for "inner" satisfactions as we explore "outer" spaces. The motor car retrieved the countryside, scrapped the inner core of the city, and created suburban megalopolis. Invention is the mother of necessities, old and new.

Literacy Created Both Science and Causality

THE ROYAL DIVORCE OF THOUGHT AND FEELING.
[JAMES JOYCE]

Twenty-five centuries ago the Greeks invented Nature by abstracting it from total existence. They elevated their cosmos as an ordered figure upon the old ground of "chaotic" change. Since then, Western philosophers have looked upon the abstract figure of Greek Nature as their territory — an artificial ground which they have cut into conceptual figures that hide existence. Harold Innis was the first to demonstrate that Greek ability to separate "thinking" from "being" was due to their alphabetic writing. In *The Bias of Communication* [4] Innis traces this causal process through the gradual shift of sensory bias from the preliterate audile-tactile to the literate visual modes of perception. Literacy became synonymous with Western civilization that divorced "subject" from "object" and thought from feeling, just as the dominant metaphors of mechanism widened the separation of "cause" and "effect."

In his analysis of *The Logic of Scientific Discovery* [5] Karl R. Popper states:

> The "principle of causality" is the assertion that any event whatsoever can be causally explained — that it can be deductively predicted. According to the way in which one interprets the word "can" in this assertion, it will be either tautological (analytic), or else an assertion about reality (synthetic). For if "can" means that it is always logically possible to construct a causal explanation, then the assertion is tautological, since for any prediction whatsoever we can always find universal statements and initial conditions from which the prediction is derivable. (Whether these universal statements have been tested and corroborated in other cases is of course quite a different question.) If, however, "can" is meant to signify that the world is governed by strict laws, that it is so constructed that every specific event is an instance of a universal regularity or law, then the assertion is admittedly synthetic. But in this case it is not falsifiable, . . . I shall, therefore, neither adopt nor reject the "principle of causality"; I shall be content simply to exclude it, as "metaphysical," from the sphere of science.
>
> I shall, however, propose a methodological rule which corresponds so closely to the "principle of causality" that the latter might be regarded as its metaphysical version. It is the simple rule that we are not to abandon the search for universal

4 Toronto, 1964.
5 New York, 1959.

> laws and for a coherent theoretical system, nor ever give up our attempts to explain causally any kind of event we can describe. This rule guides the scientific investigator in his work.

While exhorting scientists to continue "explaining" Nature as if by "causality," Popper proceeds to categorize it out of science into metaphysics via the "Vienna Circle." Unaware of the processes involved in discovering and transforming existence, Popper fails to consider the effects upon man himself of his own "hardware" and "software" extensions. There is unanimity among historians in presenting their subjects as figures without grounds.

Science Organizes Knowledge, Not Ignorance, Labels Rather than Processes

LOVE MY LABEL LIKE MYSELF. [JAMES JOYCE]

Thomas Kuhn explains how scientists operate: One of the reasons why normal science seems to progress so rapidly is that its practitioners concentrate on "problems that only their own lack of ingenuity should keep them from solving." [6] And later, "Discovery comes with the awareness of anomaly, i.e. with the recognition that nature has somehow violated the paradigm-induced expectations that govern *normal science*." [7] Kuhn shows that the "paradigm of science" is the "medium" that transforms its "content" into normal science. But he remains oblivious of the much wider hidden ground of Western culture — the unconscious assumptions of visual psychic bias. He is unaware that the user is necessarily the "content" of any situation. Whereas the

---

6 Thomas S. Kuhn, *The Structure of Scientific Revolutions* (Chicago, 1962), p. 37.

7 Ibid., p. 52.

alphabet intensified by print "wrote off" existence, the "paradigm of science" has now become the cause of "normal science." Experiments designed to confirm the old normally conceal the new. *The medium is the message.*

George Bernard Shaw once tartly remarked that "every profession is a conspiracy against the laity." And Michael Polanyi recently added that "the principle of mutual control" ensures public recognition only to normal scientists, that is, conventional wisdom only. While supporting any scientist against every layman, "scientists watch over each other." Their hidden assumption is that a "field of systematic progress exists" — a never-ending upward progression from one step of the ladder of scientific knowledge to the next. Scientists defend their "cause" by mediated consensus — a "Skinner-box" that reinforces the "message." The new conventional wisdom is being seen, if not heard, at the annual convention. [8]

Erwin Chargaff describes the dilemma facing every pioneer — "either to *understand* the world or to *explain* it":

> The natural scientist is often faced with a series of observations, a set of phenomena, into which he attempts subsequently to introduce some sort of chronological or causal order. He determines several points and connects them to a curve; he measures certain values in a number of samples and estimates the averages and deviations; he constructs a reaction chain or postulates a cycle: whatever he does, there remains much darkness between the few points of light. Whether he emphasizes the light or dwells on the obscurities will depend upon his temperament, but even more upon the temper of the times and upon a form of everchanging vogue or fashion which acts as a censor forbidding him to be

---

8 *The Tacit Dimension* (New York, 1967), pp. 71-72.

ahead by more than one or two steps. If he runs too fast, he disappears from our sight; if he goes too slowly, he joins the 18th century. For most people, this is not a problem: they are where all the others are. [9]

Professor Chargaff is here illuminating the obsession of scientists with concepts. And Donald A. Schon notes that "the tendency either to obscurantize or to explain away novelty reflects the great difficulty of explaining it. The difficulty comes in large part from our inclination, with things and thought alike, to take an after-the-fact view." [10] What the scientist normally sees is either a replay of past scientific experience or an up-and-coming threat in his "rear-view mirror." Coming events cast their shadows before them? Don't look back; they may be gaining on you!

Causality as Probe, Not Program

Mario Bunge concludes his study of causality by saying:

> There is no necessary relation between causality and prediction, any more than there is between causality and explanation. [11]. . . The causal principle reflects or reconstructs only a few aspects of determination. Reality is much too rich to be compressible once and for all into a framework of categories elaborated during an early stage of rational knowledge, which consequently cannot account for the whole variety of types of determination . . . What has been rejected in this book is not the principle of causation, but its unlimited extrapolation, as asserted by the doctrine of causalism, or causal determinism. . . . The causal principle is, in short, . . . a general hypothesis subsumed under the universal principle of determinacy, and having an approximate validity in its proper domain. [12]

---

9 E. Chargaff, "Preface to a Grammar of Biology," Science 172, no 3984 (May, 1971): 638.

10 *Displacement of Concepts* (London, 1963).

11 Bunge, *Causality: The Place of the Causal Principle in Modern Science* (New York, 1970), p. 332.

12 Ibid., pp. 352-53.

The "causality" concept may serve either as a "package" for old experience or as a "probe" for new knowledge. The meaning of "causality" is determined, not by definition as an isolated figure, but by what it does in re-cognizing process patterns in the ground of existence.

Causality Is Tested by Experience as Percept, Not Concept

To most men, experience is like the stern lights of a ship, which illumine only the track it has passed. [SAMUEL T. COLERIDGE]

Mario Bunge explains that, according to Hegel, "cause and effect are but the two poles of the interaction category, which 'realizes the causal relation in its complete development.' Besides, in Hegel's system of objective idealism, the category of interaction enjoyed an ontological status, whereas Kant had treated it, alongside the remaining categories, as a purely epistemological element, and even as prior to experience. . . . Hegel held nature in contempt." [13] Karl Marx and Friederich Engels, who were Hegel's pupils, stood on his toes rather than on his shoulders. They turned Hegelian dialectics upside down by postulating the primacy of "matter-in-motion" asymptotically reflected by mental processes. Their ambitious aim was "not merely to *understand* the world but to *change* it." They proclaimed human "experience" as the sole arbiter and the ultimate test of any "truth" whatever. But in "testing" their "truths" via dialectical materialism, they ignored the hidden ground underlying all their figures of "experience" — the visual assumptions of Western "sciences" and "humanities" alike.

---

13 Bunge, *Causality: The Place of the Causal Principle in Modern Science* (New York, 1970), pp. 161, 201.

In his *Dialectics of Nature*, Engels outlines the Marxian concept of causality:

> The first thing that strikes us in considering matter in motion is the interconnection of the individual motions of separate bodies, their *being determined* by one another. But not only do we find that a particular motion is followed by another, we find also that we can evoke a particular motion by setting up the conditions in which it takes place in nature, indeed that we can produce motions which do not occur at all in nature (industry), at least not in this way, and that we can give these motions a predetermined direction and extent. In *this way*, by the *activity of human beings*, the idea of *causality* becomes established, the idea that one motion is the *cause* of another. True, the regular sequence of certain natural phenomena can by itself give rise to the idea of causality: the heat and light that come with the sun; but this affords no proof, and to that extent Hume's skepticism was correct in saying that a regular *post hoc* can never establish a *propter hoc*. But *the activity of human beings forms the test of causality*. If we bring the sun's rays to a focus by means of a lens and make them act like the rays of an ordinary fire, we thereby prove that the heat comes from the sun. If we bring together in a rifle the priming, the explosive charge, and the bullet and then fire it, we count upon the effect known in advance from previous experience, because we can follow in all its details the whole process of ignition, combustion, explosion by the sudden conversion into gas and pressure of the gas on the bullet. And here the sceptic cannot even say that because of previous experience it does not follow that it will be the same next time. For, as a matter of fact, it does sometimes happen that it is *not* the same, that the priming or the gunpowder fails to work, that the barrel bursts, etc. But it is precisely this which *proves* causality instead of refuting it, because we can find out the cause of each such deviation from the rule by appropriate investigation: chemical decomposition of the priming, dampness, etc., of the gunpowder, defect in the barrel, etc., etc., so that here the *test of causality* is so to say a *double* one.

Natural science, like philosophy, has hitherto entirely neglected the influence of men's activity on their thought; both know only nature on the one hand and thought on the other. But it is *precisely the alteration of nature by men, not solely nature as such, which is the most essential and immediate basis of human thought, and it is in the measure that man has learned to change nature that his intelligence has increased.* The naturalistic conception of history, as found, for instance, to a greater or lesser extent in Draper and other scientists, as if nature exclusively reacts on man, and natural conditions everywhere exclusively determined his historical development, is therefore one-sided and *forgets that man also reacts on nature, changing it, and creating new conditions of existence for himself.* There is damned little left of "nature" as it was in Germany at the time when the Germanic peoples immigrated into it. The earth's surface, climate, vegetation, fauna, and the human beings themselves have continually changed, and all this owing to human activity, while the changes of nature in Germany which have occurred in the process of time without human interference are incalculably small. [14]

And he continues:

Reciprocal action is the first thing that we encounter when we consider matter in motion as a whole from the standpoint of modern natural science. We see a series of forms of motion, mechanical motion, heat, light, electricity, magnetism, chemical union and decomposition, transitions of states of aggregation, organic life, all of which, if *at present* we *still* make an exception of organic life, pass into one another, mutually determine one another, are in one place cause and in another effect, the sum-total of the motion in all its changing forms remaining the same (Spinoza: *substance is causa sui* — strikingly expresses the reciprocal action). Mechanical motion becomes transformed into heat, electricity, magnetism, light, etc., and *vice versa*. Thus natural science confirms . . . that reciprocal action is the true *causa finalis* of things. We cannot go back further than to knowledge of this reciprocal action, for the very reason that there is nothing behind to know.[15]

---

14 New York, n.d., pp. 170-72.

"This music is worse than it sounds," for it is played literally by *eye* without *ear*. Although its epistemology is dialectical, its ontology still rests on abstract Greek Nature. Marx and Engels saw conflicts of old figures as creating grounds for each other while they remained oblivious of the new information surround that had transformed their assumptions. They were attempting to *match* the concepts of an earlier age to the experience newly visible in the "rear-view-mirror" of the 19th century. They were unaware that *percepts of existence always lie behind concepts of Nature*. Their hidden hang-up was the visual bias of all "objectivity," whether "materialist" or "idealist." They also ignored the acoustic "message of the birds" — the output of any process, biological or psychic, always differs qualitatively from the input. There are no "through-puts" or connections between processes but only gaps or interfaces for "keeping in touch" with "where the action is." When the "play" between the wheel and the axle ends, so does the wheel. While the "subjectivist" puts on the world as his own clothes, the "objectivist" supposes that he can stand naked "out of this world." The ideal of the rationalist philosophers still persists: to achieve an inclusive "science of the sciences." But such a "science" would be a monster of preconceived figures minus unperceived grounds. No "objective" dialectics of Nature or of science as visually ex-plainable can stand up to a resonant interface with the existential. For "testing the truth" is not merely matching by congruence or classification; it is making sense out of the totality of experience — a process of pattern re-cognition that requires not only concepts but active perception by all the senses. Today, as "hardware" is transmuted into pure information by the process of "etherialization," the "inner" and the "outer" merge — thinking becomes doing.

---

15 New York, n.d., p. 173

The "Stereophonic" Perspective of Ear and Eye

But at my back I alwais hear
Times winged Charriot hurrying near:
And yonder all before us lye
Desarts of vast Eternity.
[ANDREW MARVELL, To His Coy Mistress]

Polonius: What do you read, my lord?
Hamlet: Words, words, words.
[WILLIAM SHAKESPEARE, Hamlet, 2.2]

In the 16th century, as words went "visual" they lost their "resoun" or metamorphic resonance and became mere "rabble." Only "artists" like William Shakespeare and Andrew Marvell were aware of the "double perspective" of hearing behind and seeing ahead. Scientists like Robert Boyle turned away from ancient books "to get in touch" again through ancient crafts. Their successors went from libraries to laboratories and pushed on to "reason" without "rhyme." Early perspective was toward the viewer and began to recede only in the Renaissance. Today television begins perspective back toward the viewer again. The reversal of sensory stress from *eye* to *ear* via media is perceived by "artists" like James Joyce and T. S. Eliot as an opportunity for consciously retrieving reason, rhyme, and rhythm:

STOP
LOOK
LISTEN

The visual metaphors of science have had the effect of translating totalities of process relations into mere connections between separate phenomena, or things. John Stuart Mill wrote: "The Law of Causation ... is but the familiar truth that invariability of succession is found by observation to obtain between every fact in nature and some other fact which has preceded it.... The invariable antecedent is termed the cause; the invariable consequent, the effect." [16] Pushed to extreme, the fragmented figures of abstract Nature exclude the ground of actual nature. But always the action is in the gap. There are no "things," only processes.

Whereas "reality" in the 19th century was to match the old, "reality" in the 20th century is to make the new. Since Werner Heisenberg and Linus Pauling, [17] the only remaining material bond is resonance. All physical, psychic, and social processes merge in constant play and replay. There are no more spectators in lab or life, only participants in the Global Electric Theatre. Sputnik created a new proscenium arch that transformed our awareness of planet Polluto — a limited figure against the ground of limitless space. The Apollo age has scrapped Greek Nature as we assume full responsibility for orchestrating our total environment on human scales beyond ideologies.

Effects Precede Causes

THE CHILD IS FATHER TO THE MAN.
[WILLIAM WORDSWORTH]

The father and the family make the child, just as the child remakes them in a continuing process. Like families, all grounds

---

16 *A System of Logic*, 9th ed. (London, 1875), p. 376.

17 In *The Nature of the Chemical Bond and the Structures of Molecules and Crytals: An Introduction to Modern Chemistry*, 3rd ed. (Ithaca, N. Y., 1967), Pauling establishes that the chemical bond is not a mere connection but a "stabilization of the system of resonance energy."

are a totality of cumulative effects that continually gell into figures as causes. "When the time is ripe" in any process, the effects as ground have preceded the cause as figures. *"Causality" is a process pattern, exposed by discovery or imposed by invention.* The effects are consciously made accessible either through discovery or invention as new causes, both "hardware" and "software." For example, while tracing the development of American agriculture, Sigfried Giedion observes that "phenomena often regarded solely as the outcome of mechanization had already appeared before the mechanization took effect." [18] Similarly, many of the effects of the telephone had been anticipated by the general speedup of information that centered in the telegraph. The effects of "wireless" were anticipated by earlier technologies of wire and cable. Road traffic had been steadily accelerating before the advent of the railroad. A general environmental speedup preceded the development of the airways. The new effects through new uses of any innovation are realized only after it becomes obsolescent through fresh innovation. The old hidden ground then emerges as a new rear-view figure for all to see. Computers are still serving mainly as agents to sustain precomputer effects.

In the broader context of *The Hidden Face*, Ida F. Goerres observes that "those who experience great historical changes at first hardly notice them, only the fact that they are being dragged along willy-nilly; some time must always elapse before such changes pierce to the deeper levels of consciousness and engender new attitudes, new modes of behaviour." [19] Conceptual formulation, whether in "software" or "hardware," always lags behind "where it's at."

---

18 *Mechanization Takes Command* (New York, 1948), p. 168.

19 New York, 1959, p. 24.

Effects Are Perceived Whereas Causes are Conceived

Unable to explore actual processes perceptually from every side, the conceptual man apprehends only visual goals. For example, the conventional ideas of "evolution" and "technology" are illusions engendered by the visual bias of literate cultures. Such cultures translated the "chain of being" metaphor from the astral to the biological plane. For the use of the "missing link" idea we are indebted to a missing inventor. So far nobody has appeared as originator of this phrase. The gap created by the "missing link" has sparked more exploration and discovery than the established links in "connected" science. Conceptual choices, like "natural selection," can come only after the fact. The "origins" of all species vanish in rear-view perspectives, while the music goes round and round.

Causality is Not Merely Reciprocal Action but Complementary Process

Nils Bohr's complementarity that represents "atomic" interactions as both "acoustic" waves and "visual" particles is exemplified by every process involving the continuous interplay of simultaneous actions. (All "elementary particles" are packaged ignorance.) Aristotle's "pairs," where one process is always the privation of another, were also familiar to the Chinese sage Wang Fu (A. D. 90-165): "Poverty arises from wealth, weakness derives from power./Order engenders disorder, and security insecurity." [20] That is, affluence breeds poverty (not physical hardship) and learning causes ignorance (not less information), just as matter creates

20 Cited by Etienne Balasz in *Chinese Civilization and Bureaucracy: Variations on a Theme* (New Haven, Conn., 1967).

space (not void). Such complementarity of figure-ground appears as a causal relation in all "prepackaged" processes. *Complementarity is the process whereby effects become causes.* Today, as causes and effects merge instantaneously, the new common ground is neither container nor category but the vastness of space via media.

Explanations East or West?

WHAT WE CANNOT SPEAK ABOUT WE MUST CONFINE TO SILENCE.
[L. WITTGENSTEIN]

What most scientists still fail to perceive is the "visual" bias of logical inference imposed by Western civilization itself. What constitutes a fact or an adequate explanation? Mario Bunge writes:

> Most scientists are prepared to grant that the chief theoretical (that is, nonpragmatic) aim of scientific research is to answer, in an intelligible, exact, and testable way, five kinds of questions, namely, those beginning with *what* (or *how*), *where*, *when*, *whence*, and *why*. . . . The Five W's of Science. (Only radical empiricists deny that science has an explanatory function, and restrict the task of scientific research to the description and prediction of observable phenomena.) Also, most scientists would agree that all five W's are gradually (and painfully) being answered through the establishment of scientific *laws*, that is, general hypotheses abut the patterns of being and becoming. [21]

The poet Ezra Pound understood that the telegraphic mosaic of news items and headlines was an organization of experience that bridged the ancient Oriental and Western forms. In his *ABC of Reading*,[22] Pound cites an essay by Ernest Fenollosa:

---

21 Bunge, p. 248.

22 New York, 1960, pp. 19-22 (New Directions Paperback no. 89).

In Europe, if you ask a man to define anything, his definition always moves away from the simple things that he knows perfectly well, it recedes into an unknown region of remoter and progressively remoter abstraction.

Thus if you ask him what red is, he says it is a "colour."

If you ask him what a colour is, he tells you it is a vibration or reflection of light, or a division of the spectrum. And if you ask him what vibration is, he tells you it is a mode of energy, or something of that sort, until you arrive at a modality of being, or non-being, or at any rate you get in beyond your depth, and beyond his depth . . . . But when the Chinaman wanted . . . to define red . . . how did he go about it?

He . . . put together the abbreviated pictures of

ROSE CHERRY

IRON RUST FLAMINGO

. . . the Chinese "word" or ideogram for red is based on something everyone *knows*.

Explanations that ignore the perceptual complementarity of *eye* and *ear* lead to conceptual conflict — the divorce of "rhyme and reason." "I have often seen it said," repeats the specialist. "Speak that I may see thee," said the seer.

Every language creates an all-pervasive hidden environment of services. And words themselves are metaphors (Greek *metapherein*: carry across) that transform meaning by translating one form of being into another. The semanticist ideal — one word for one meaning — has already been achieved by "yes-or-no" computer languages. Whereas computer programmers try to reduce the infinite variety of the world to the two-bit wit of their machines, "artists" like James Joyce can create universes of resonant meaning out of two words: the "orb urbs" and the "urb orbs."

Making Sense

POETRY CAN COMMUNICATE BEFORE IT IS UNDERSTOOD. [T. S. ELIOT]

The *eye* makes a "visual space structure" with individual points of view or centers and definite margins or boundaries — everything in its proper place and time. Each of our senses makes its own space, but no sense can function in isolation. Only as sight relates to touch, or kinesthesia, or sound, can the eye see. In isolation, the visual sense presents an immediate blur — all ground minus figures. The bridging of the senses creates an interface of figure-ground relations that make sense. Making sense is never matching or mere one-to-one correspondence which is an assumption of visual bias. For the *ear* makes an "acoustic space structure" with centers everywhere and margins nowhere, like a musical surround or the boundless universe. Making sense involves "unified sensibility" or *synesthesia*, as E. H. Gombrich explains in *Art and Illusion*:

What is called "synesthesia," the splashing over of impressions from one sense modality to another, is a fact to which all languages testify. They work both ways — from sight to sound and from sound to sight. We speak of loud colors or of bright sounds, and everyone knows what we mean. Nor are the ear and the eye the only senses that are thus converging to a common center. There is touch in such terms as "velvety voice" and "a cold light," taste with "sweet harmonies" of colors or sounds, and so on through countless permutations.... Representation is never a replica. The forms of art, ancient and modern, are not duplications of what the artist has in mind any more than they are duplications of what he sees in the outer world. In both cases they are renderings within an acquired medium, a medium grown up through tradition and skill – that of the artist and that of the beholder.... Synesthesia concerns relationships.[23]

Relevant to the great gap between program "content" and the effect of the medium itself is the approach to the image in J. Isaac's *Background of Modern Poetry*: " 'The exact word,' says Mr. Aldington, 'does not mean the word which exactly describes the object itself, it means the exact word which brings the effect of that object before the reader as it presented itself to the poet's mind at the time of writing the poem.' "[24] Apropos the linguistic studies of N. Chomsky, Thomas S. Kuhn, philosopher of science, was recently cited by the *Listener* on "what people are prepared to accept as facts at one point cease to be and new things are regarded as facts."[25] Our studies of media as environments that alter patterns of perception and sensibility are intended to develop awareness of the process by which "new things" come to be regarded as "facts." These "new facts" concern the message or effects of new media as hidden environments. These effects are not the "content" of the media. The content is always the "hypocrite lecteur" (or *auditeur*). This is the central fact missing from the speculations of Noam Chomsky concerning the verbal universe. Languages are not programs but environments which are hidden from the young learner, and to which, like fish to water, he relates

23 New York, 1965, pp. 366-70.

24 New York, n.d., p. 45.

25 July 27, 1971, p. 142.

synesthetically, using all his faculties at once. After childhood the senses specialize via the channels of dominant technologies and social weaponries. Electric channels of information have the effect of reducing (or elevating) people to the discarnate status of instant information.

The Artist Precedes the Scientist

The first principle of evidence is that things have to be approached on their own terms if any understanding is to be attained. Edgar Allan Poe was the first to stress the need to begin with effects and to work backwards, in poetry and in detective fiction alike. Just as Poe provided clues for ascending from *The Maelstrom*, Beckett replays not waiting, but the effects of the experience of waiting, in *Waiting for Godot*. In *Four Quartets* T. S. Eliot studies effects as causes: "In my end is my beginning." And Wyndham Lewis noted that "the artist is engaged in writing a detailed history of the future because, 'older than the fish,' he alone can live in the inclusive present." In symbolist art, connections are deliberately pulled out in order to involve the public in a creative role. In symbolist statement, the ground is suppressed in order to highlight the figure. A boot lying on a highway is a symbol, a tire is not, for the medium can reverse the roles of producer and consumer by making the reader or audience not only the "content" but the comaker of the work. Movies and television are antithetic.

When we say "the medium is the message," we suppress the fact that the user or audience or cognitive agent is both the "content" and maker of the experience, in order to highlight the effects of the medium or the hidden environment or ground of the experience. The 19th century, as the first great consumer age, suppressed the function of the user and the public as cognitive agent and producer. The pre-Raphaelites at least strove to overcome the passive consumer bias of an industrial time by stressing the role of work and crafts in art and society. They tried to have some relevance to their time by playing down the consumer role and scorning the easy package method that had grown up in the arts and industry alike. In his time, John Donne strove for relevance to his "hypocrite lecteurs" by constructing for them a broken and discontinuous discourse. He was seeking nonlineal and non-19th-century effects "to trouble the understanding, to displace, and discompose and disorder the judgement . . . or to empty it of former apprehensions, and to shake beliefs, with which it had possessed itself before, and then, when it is thus melted, to poure it into new molds, when it is thus mollified, to stamp and imprint new forms, and new opinions in it." Donne's "Attic" or "curt" and broken style not only ruffled the feathers of the 19th-century establishment, but appeals to contemporary minds in our own century.

In 1903, W. B. Yeats, meditating on the "emotion of multitude," explained that it is achieved by a discontinuous parallel between two actions; "I have been wondering why I dislike the clear and logical construction which seems necessary if one is to succeed on the modern stage . . . . The Greek drama has got the emotion of multitude from its chorus . . . to witness as it were, some well ordered fable . . . . The Shakespearean drama gets the emotion of multitude out of the sub-plot which copies the main plot, much as a shadow upon the wall copies one's body in the firelight. We think of King Lear less as the history of one man and his sorrows than as the history of a whole evil time." Depth awareness is created by parallel suggestion, not by connected statement. Yeats's observation can also be found in Bacon, who writes on the modes of aphorism as contrasted with "writing in Method," in his *Advancement of Learning*: "Aphorisms, representing a knowledge broken, do invite men to inquire farther; whereas Methods, carrying the show of a total, do secure men, as if they were at farthest." Even the ad agencies know that to sell a car or a coat they must present the satisfactions in figure-ground relationship that will create the desired psychic effects. They would not show a coat in relation to naked natives nor a car in a world without roads. The 19th-century consumer preference is not relevant to the electric age of quantum physics, even though our media bureaucracies continue to produce mainly consumer packages. But every specialist has a stake in his own knowledge, just as every conventional man has the right to defend his own ignorance.

Causality as Making the New

What Western philosophers, right, left, and center, have continued to ignore is that *matching* the old excludes *making* the new. Concepts always follow percepts. In fact they are a kind of ossification of percepts — endlessly repeated percepts which frequently obscure invention and innovation.

The entire obsession of our age with *existentialism* has been based on the awareness that concept is not percept. One can have numerous classifications that do not correspond to one's actual experience. We are often smothered in images of ourselves and of others that do not correspond to "presences." The Western world has built up a vast apparatus of classifications as a means of controlling and harmonizing experience. These have tended to be colossal systems of concepts which prevent us from direct encounter with ourselves and our world: they constitute the "rear-view mirror." But "existentialism" pushed to extreme as a figure loses touch with the ground of existence itself.

The Renaissance made a clean sweep of the vast methodologies and dialectics of scholastic disputation. Today, we are making a clean sweep of all the merely private points of view achieved through five centuries of intense individualism. Inevitably, in these cathartic conditions, many babies are thrown out with little bath water. Enormous destruction seems to accompany such periods of discovery and innovation. The ordinary flood of effects that pour from ill-conceived courses of action swamp perception.

Scientific "objectivity," like Othello's "ocular proof," is an optical illusion of truth. The testimony of the blind Frenchman Jacques Lusseyran is relevant here:

> When I came across the myth of objectivity in certain modern writers, it made me angry. So there was only one world for these people, the same for everyone. And all the other worlds were to be counted as illusions left over from the past. Or why not call them by their name — hallucinations? I had to learn to my cost how wrong they were.
>
> From my experience I knew that it was enough to take from a man a memory here, an association there, to deprive him of hearing or sight, for the world to undergo immediate transformation, and for another world, entirely different but entirely

coherent to be born. Another world? Not really. The same world, rather, but seen from another angle, and counted in entirely new measures. When this happened, all the hierarchies they called objective were turned upside down, scattered to the four winds, not even like theories but like whims.[26]

"Objectivity" is achieved by matching new observations with old concepts by specialist observers doubly isolated from existence by abstract Nature on the one hand, and controlled laboratory environments on the other. No dog from the street will behave in accordance with the stimulus-response figures of "conditioned reflexes" until conditioned by a Pavlovian ground. The laboratory is the hidden environment of effects that make the causes possible.

Truth is never a label; it is not something we match. Truth is something we make with all our senses in a conscious process of remaking the world as the world remakes us physically, psychically, and socially.

Predicting What Has Already Happened By Being the First to Perceive It

Displacing percepts is the role of the artist. The artist in any field is the person who anticipates the effects in his own times, both of new knowledge and of his own actions. The art of remaking the world eternally new is achieved by careful and deliberate dislocation of ordinary perceptions. Even the surrealist had this ambition — to attain a fresh vision of the world by the juxtaposition of ordinary things, for example, the "fur-lined teacup" and "Mona Lisa's moustache." Scientists make their dis-

26 *And There Was Light* (Boston, 1963) pp. 143-44.

coveries as "artists," not specialists. Such scientists construct experiments as "works of art" to probe the environment. But anyone with enough vitality to confront the actual through direct perception can predict the future by noting what has already happened. For the future of the future is the present.

The breakdown or hang-up is always in the connection, whereas the breakthrough or discovery is inside the problem itself, not outside but "in the gap." Breakdown is the old cause in action, the extension of the old figure to the new ground. Breakthrough is the effect of understanding as the new cause. The solution is a figure that we can discover by organizing our ignorance and swarming over the ground. This process is encapsulated in the myth of Hercules in the Augean stables.

Causality on Both Sides of the Looking Glass

As the mathematician Charles Dodgson (Lewis Carroll), romping with *Alice in Wonderland*, explains while playing hitherside of the glass in Logic-land "'Contrariwise,' continued Tweedledee, 'if it was so, it might be; and if it were so, it would be; but as it isn't, it ain't. That's logic.'" And while playing thitherside in Echo-land: "Now, *here*, you see, it takes all the running *you* can do, to stay in the same place. If you want to get somewhere else, you must run at least twice as fast as that!" Today, all barriers have gone with the ether as we live on both sides of the looking glass.

Understanding is Neither a Point of View nor a Value Judgment

Lewis Carroll makes inventories of effects as causes that relate modes of dynamic perception. They are neither definitions of concepts nor expressions of opinion, since all patterns of perception merge and metamorphose in the very act of exploration and discovery. They avoid value judgments, and serve as guides to insight and to comprehension through *re-cognition* of the *dynamic structures* that occur in all processes. In replaying such patterns we are not taking any side but many sides, also the *inside*.

Today's Causality Program's Evitable Fate

At electric speeds, new direct perception of existence bypasses old die-hard concepts of Nature. We can now anticipate the effects — both services and disservices — before allowing the causes to develop. We no longer merely choose options, we make them. We can invent the remedies for both fortune and misfortune. Today, causing and explaining and predicting merge while teacher-student, consumer-producer, and audience-actor unite in new roles for the Global Electric Theatre. The future is not what it used to be; neither is causality, for thought travels much faster and farther than light.

The Argument: Causality in the Electric World
Marshall McLuhan - Unbound (03)

ISBN: 1-58423-051-7
Library of Congress Control Number 2005927213

Marshall McLuhan Unbound Project Editors
Eric McLuhan, W. Terrence Gordon

Published in United States in October 2005 by
Gingko Press, Inc.
5768 Paradise Drive, Suite J • Corte Madera, CA 94925
(415) 924-9615 • Fax (415) 924-9608
email: books@gingkopress.com
http://www.gingkopress.com

© Barrington Nevitt and The Estate of Mashall McLuhan.

Introduction to "The Argument: Causality in the Electric World" © W. Terrence Gordon

Design, packaging and production: Die Gestalten Verlag, Berlin
Layout and Typography: onlab, Berlin
Fonts: *Dolly* by Underware, *Bullet* by House Industries
Production: Martin Bretschneider, Vinzenz Geppert
Art direction: Robert Klanten

Made in Germany

All rights reserved. No part of this essay may be used or reproduced in any manner whatsoever without written permission from the publisher except in the case of brief quotations embodied in critical articles and reviews. For information address Gingko Press.